★ POP CULTURE BIOS

REBEL

WILSON

FROM STAND-UP LAUGHS TO BOX-OFFICE SMASH

HEATHER E. SCHWARTZ

Lerner Publications Company
MINNEAPOLIS

Thank you to my cheery and
cooperative baby son,
Griffin Schwartz

Lerner Publications Company
A division of Lerner Publishing Group, Inc.
241 First Avenue North
Minneapolis, MN 55401 USA

For reading levels and more information, look up this title at
www.lernerbooks.com.

Library of Congress Cataloging-in-Publication Data

Schwartz, Heather E.
    Rebel Wilson : from stand-up laughs to box-office smash /
Heather E. Schwartz.
        p.   cm. — (Pop culture bios)
    Includes index.
    ISBN 978–1–4677–1443–3 (lib. bdg. : alk. paper)
    ISBN 978–1–4677–2503–3 (eBook)
    1. Wilson, Rebel—Juvenile literature. 2. Comedians—United
States—Juvenile literature. 3. Actors—United States—Juvenile
literature. I. Title.
PN2287.W4935S35 2014
792.02'8092—dc23 [B]   2013022646

Manufactured in the United States of America
1 – PC – 12/31/13

INTRODUCTION

Rebel accepts the award for Choice Movie: Comedy Actress at the 2013 Teen Choice Awards.

TEEN CHOICE 2013

From the stage at the 2013 MTV Movie Awards, Rebel Wilson smiles as the audience claps and cheers. Her black gown sparkles. This is her moment. She's ready to work it to address an issue close to her heart: body image.

Rebel takes to the mic. She tells the crowd how she has learned to love herself. Self-acceptance is critical, she says, and people should love themselves regardless of their size or shape. It's a fantastic message.

Rebel takes the stage to host the 2013 MTV Movie Awards on April 14, 2013.

But then, just as she's begun to speak, the top of her dress starts to slide down. Yikes! Pretty soon, Rebel's big moment seems to have turned into an embarrassing nightmare. But Rebel's fans need not feel bad for her for long. Why? This "mishap" is totally planned! Rebel did it to give her audience a good laugh. The skin underneath

Rebel performs a skit as part of her award show hosting duties.

her dress is covered by a flesh-toned bodysuit. And her speech? Well, she means every word of that— but she makes it funny too. After years of honing her skills, Rebel knows how to captivate an audience, make a serious point, and get some laughs all at the same time. No joke about it: this star is a comedian to the very core.

Rebel scored a few MTV movie awards for her performance in the movie *Pitch Perfect*.

Rebel (LEFT) and her sister Liberty

CHAPTER ONE

AUSTRALIAN UPBRINGING

Rebel grew up in Sydney, Australia.

Rebel Wilson's name perfectly reflects who she is today. She's funny and fearless. She's outspoken and quirky. But growing up in Australia, she wasn't known as a rule breaker. Far from it. In fact, she's described herself as shy and studious. She didn't like talking to people. She didn't even like answering questions in class. Back then, she went by Melanie Elizabeth, her two middle names. That was a much better fit.

Rebel's parents had unusual jobs. They were both dog handlers—people who specialize in presenting dogs for judges at dog shows. Every weekend, the Wilson family trekked to dog shows with their beagles. Constantly meeting new people was a challenge for young Rebel. But at least she had her sibs—Liberty, Ryot, and Annachi—for company. Plus, each new stop on their trail was a chance to people watch. Rebel liked that part of her unusual lifestyle.

WHAT'S IN A NAME?

Born February 3, 1986, Rebel Melanie Elizabeth Wilson was named after a girl who sang at her parents' wedding. Although Rebel wasn't rebellious in her early years, she eventually grew to be a young woman who's not afraid to break the rules!

Dog handlers prepare their pooches for presentation at the Westminster Kennel Club dog show. Rebel's parents worked as dog handlers.

Hidden Talent

When Rebel was fourteen, her mom had an idea. How about an acting class to help her shed her shyness? Rebel was far from thrilled. On the way there, she cried until her face turned red. But there was no getting out of it. Her mom dropped her off, and Rebel was stranded.

When the teacher asked her name, she knew she had to answer. But just speaking her name aloud seemed scary! Rebel could think of only one thing to do. She started speaking in an American accent. She felt less shy if she pretended to be someone else. It was only her first day of acting class, and Rebel was already acting!

AUDITION =
a tryout for a part

High School and Beyond

That acting class was just the start of Rebel's adventures in performing. The class built up her confidence. Soon she was trying out for—and nailing!—auditions for school plays.

But acting wasn't the only thing Rebel liked to do. During high school, she played tennis, hockey, and basketball. She sang in choir. She also did well in the classroom, earning top-notch grades.

NOW THAT'S DEDICATION!

In high school, Rebel was in the musical *Fiddler on the Roof*. During one performance, she fell off part of the set! She sprained her ribs and wrist. But she still came back for the next night's performance.

Since Rebel was a smart student, she was looking for a challenge after high school. She applied to law school and was easily accepted. But first, she decided to travel to South Africa. She wanted to try something new, and a trip to another country seemed like just the thing.

Rebel visited South Africa as a Rotary International Youth Ambassador. Pictured below is its capital city of Johannesburg.

Unfortunately, Rebel came down with a nasty case of malaria in South Africa. She was so sick, she started hallucinating. To this day, she remembers some of her stranger hallucinations. In one, she saw herself at the Oscars winning an award!

MALARIA =
a serious illness that causes chills and fever

Even though it was only in her mind, the way Rebel felt when she thought she won an Oscar stayed with her for a long time. When she recovered, she decided the hallucination had been a sign. She'd still go to law school, she decided. But she'd also explore acting and see how far she could get in the field.

HALLUCINATING =
seeing things that aren't there. A high fever can cause hallucinations.

CHAPTER TWO

CREATING A CAREER

When she got back to Australia, Rebel began studying at the Australian Theatre for Young People (ATYP). She also started auditioning for acting jobs. But she didn't score any major roles.

She tried talking to an agent to get career advice. But all she got was a snarky remark about her plus-size figure. Rebel was hurt by the agent's comment. But she didn't let it discourage her. In fact, she decided to explore additional avenues in the entertainment field, on top of acting. The ambitious young woman started writing her own plays.

Rebel (TOP) poses with fellow actors from the Australian Theatre for Young People in September 2002.

Since Rebel's plays were her own creation, she decided she could also choose who starred in them. She chose herself! That's when her talents started getting recognized. By the early 2000s, she'd scored a recurring role on the Australian comedy series *Pizza*. She also got the chance of a lifetime. Thanks to a scholarship through the ATYP, she was able to study acting in New York.

Rebel studied comedy while living in New York City.

SCHOLARSHIP = money given to someone to help pay for their studies

Paul Fenech (CENTER) was the creator and star of the TV series *Pizza* and the movie *Fat Pizza*.

Success led to more success. Rebel took her *Pizza* character to the big screen in the movie *Fat Pizza*. She performed as a stand-up comedian too. In addition, she got on some international TV programs, including *The World Comedy Tour: Melbourne 2005*.

In 2007, Rebel got a chance to be in a movie with American star Nicolas Cage. Her part was so tiny that the character didn't even have a name. But as Girl in Alley, she delivered her lines with an unforgettable, original style. Rebel was making her way in the acting world.

Rebel encouraged her brother, Ryot, and sister Liberty to get into show business too. She thought they'd love entertaining just as much as she does. They took her advice! The pair was on the show *The Amazing Race Australia* in 2011.

Liberty (LEFT) and Ryot (RIGHT) were eliminated in the second episode of *The Amazing Race Australia*.

Double Life

Rebel wasn't a household name yet. But she was definitely a professional actress. Still, she kept plugging away at a law degree from the University of New South Wales. She figured practicing law could be a backup career if acting didn't pan out in the long run.

Rebel studied law at the University of New South Wales.

But studying law on top of acting was a killer. To get a degree, Rebel had to make it to 80 percent of her classes. It wasn't easy for an actress who was filming at different locations. Rebel flew back and forth to attend class. She struck deals with professors to make up exams.

Although Rebel never practiced law, the hard work of law school did pay off in one way. She's able to negotiate her own acting contracts. Rebel says people are often surprised to see a woman who plays so many offbeat characters talking about the ins and outs of the law!

CONTRACT = a formal, written agreement between actors and those hiring actors

Breakout Show

In 2008, Rebel's career reached new heights when she created her own television series for an Australian network. *Bogan Pride* was a comedy about a teenage girl who struggles with obesity—a topic Rebel herself knew something about. Writing and starring in her own show was major. The series lasted only one season. Yet it was a great accomplishment for someone so new to entertainment. And as Rebel was soon to discover, even more amazing opportunities were about to come her way.

Rebel poses with her *Bogan Pride* cast mate Sally-Ann Upton (LEFT) in 2008.

WHAT A COINCIDENCE

Rebel named her *Bogan Pride* character Jennie Cragg, after the popular weight-loss program called Jenny Craig. A few years later, in 2011, Rebel became a spokesperson for the Jenny Craig company!

Rebel (BACK) in a scene from Bridesmaids

CHAPTER THREE

MAJOR PLAYER

After *Bogan Pride*, Rebel got an audition for a film called *Bridesmaids*. Rebel was thrilled. However, she soon learned that the part had gone to another actress. That news was disappointing. But Rebel got some good news too. Her talents had wowed the filmmakers so much that they couldn't let her walk away. They told her they were writing a new character into the script just for her!

Rebel was to play Brynn, a roommate of the film's main character. Brynn is quirky, and Rebel knew just how to play up those quirks. She shined on-screen and caught the attention of everyone in Hollywood.

FREE SHOW!

In 2012, Rebel got an apartment in West Hollywood. She and her roommate, *Bridesmaids* actor Matt Lucas (SHOWN AT RIGHT), liked singing show tunes from the musical *Annie* when they were at home together. A neighbor shut down their act, though, by threatening to call the police when they got a little too noisy!

Hollywood Calling

After *Bridesmaids*, Rebel's career totally took off. She played a bride in the movie *Bachelorette*. Then a filmmaker invited her to audition for the role of Fat Amy in *Pitch Perfect*. She got that part too!

Was Rebel insulted to play someone whom everyone calls fat? Not a chance. She has so much confidence that

Rebel played Fat Amy in *Pitch Perfect*. The character joins an all-girl singing group led by Anna Camp (RIGHT).

the name didn't bother her a bit. And later, Rebel felt honored to be recognized for her performance. Still, she doesn't want every character she plays to be known for her weight. She thinks playing different kinds of characters is important. That way, she won't get stereotyped as someone who plays only certain kinds of roles.

Rebel sings a solo in a scene from *Pitch Perfect*.

PITCH PERFECT AUDITION

Rebel had to show off her pipes to earn her role in *Pitch Perfect*. She sang Lady Gaga's "The Edge of Glory" and got just what she wanted— the part of Fat Amy!

Maximum Talent

Rebel wasn't in danger of being stereotyped. Her next role couldn't have been more different from the one she had in *Pitch Perfect*. This time, she played an animated character—or at least, the voice of one. She brought Raz the kangaroo to life in *Ice Age: Continental Drift*.

When Rebel wasn't acting, she put her writing skills to use. By 2013, she was writing a TV show called *Super Fun Night*. She also produces and acts in the show.

PRODUCE =
to pay for and organize the making of a project, such as a movie, a TV show, or a musical album

Rebel shares a scene with her *Super Fun Night* costars Liza Lapira (LEFT) and Lauren Ash (CENTER).

Rebel's triple dose of talent as an actress, singer, and writer keeps the star in high demand. With her brains and skill, there's no doubt she'll keep on flourishing. That's welcome news to Rebel's many fans, who can't wait to see what hilarious projects she has in store for them next!

SUPER-FUN NERDS

Rebel's newest show, *Super Fun Night*, is about three nerdy and unpopular women. She's told the media it's based on her own life. Is she only kidding? It's hard to say. But it's tough to imagine that *everyone* wouldn't love someone as awesome as Rebel!

REBEL PICS!

Rebel with Rose Bryne (LEFT) and Ellie Kemper (CENTER) at the Bridesmaids premiere.

Rebel signs autographs for fans.

Pitch Perfect
http://www.pitchperfectmovie.com
Visit the official website of *Pitch Perfect*, the hilarious musical comedy that helped make Rebel a household name.

Rebel Wilson Alumni Bio
http://www.atyp.com.au/about/alumni/rebel-wilson
The Australian Theatre for Young People is so proud of their former student! Read what they have to say about Rebel.

Rebel Wilson on IMDb
http://www.imdb.com/name/nm2313103
Visit Rebel's page on the Internet Movie Database for her full résumé, official photos, a biography, and more.

Seventeen: Rebel's Secrets to Super Confidence!
http://www.seventeen.com/entertainment/features/rebel-wilson-interview
Read five awesome tips from Rebel on how to build up your confidence.

Smith, Emly. *The Rebel Wilson Handbook.* Queensland, AU: Emereo Publishing, 2013.
Learn more about Rebel's life and rise to superstardom.

INDEX

PHOTO ACKNOWLEDGMENTS

The images in this book are used with the permission of: © Lisa Maree Williams/Getty Images, pp. 2, 22 (bottom right); © Scott Eells/Bloomberg/Getty Images, pp. 3 (top), 8 (top); © Carrie-nelson/ImageCollect, pp. 3 (bottom), 27; © Kevin Mazur/WireImage/Getty Images, p. 4 (top left); © Joe Seer/Shutterstock.com, p. 4 (top right); © Kevin Winter/Getty Images, pp. 4 (bottom), 28 (bottom left); © Kevork Djansezian/Getty Images, pp. 5, 6, 28 (top left); © Jason Merritt/Getty Images, pp. 7, 28 (right); © Christopher Howey/Dreamstime.com, p. 8 (bottom); © John Moore/Getty Images, p. 10; Advertising Archives/Courtesy Everett Collection, p. 11; © Patrick Allen/Dreamstime.com, p. 12; © Peter Carrette Archive/Getty Images, pp. 14 (left), 15; © Don Arnold/WireImage/Getty Images, pp. 14 (right), 17; © Ron Chapple Stock/Dreamstime.com, p. 16; © Andy Baker/Newspix, p. 18; © Julie Kiriacoudis/Newspix, p. 19; © KatChristie/Dreamstime.com, p. 20; © Kristian Dowling/Getty Images, p. 21; © Suzanne Hanover/Universal Pictures/Courtesy Everett Collection, p. 22 (top); © George Pimentel/Getty Images, p. 22 (bottom left); © John Shearer/WireImage/Getty Images, p. 23; © Peter Iovino/Universal Pictures/Courtesy Everett Collection, pp. 24, 25; AP Photo/ABC, Colleen Hayes, p. 26; © Brendon Thorne/Getty Images, p. 29 (top left); © Admedia/ImageCollect, p. 29 (top center); © Mike Marsland/WireImage/Getty Images, p. 29 (right); © Jason Merritt/WireImage/Getty Images, p. 29 (bottom).

Front cover: © Russ Elliot/AdMedia/ImageCollect (left); © BirdieThompson/AdMedia/ImageCollect (right).
Back cover: © Kevork Djansezian/Getty Images.

Main body text set in Shannon Std Book 12/18.
Typeface provided by Monotype Typography.